30 FRESH FLOWER DISPLAYS

Inspirational arrangements with glorious fresh flowers

ULTIMATE
EDITIONS

First published in 1996 by Ultimate Editions

© 1996 Anness Publishing Limited

Ultimate Editions is an imprint of
Anness Publishing Limited
Boundary Row Studios
1 Boundary Row
London SE1 8HP

ISBN 1 86035 181 6

Distributed in Canada by Book Express, an imprint of
Raincoast Books Distribution Limited

Publisher: Joanna Lorenz
Project Editor: Fiona Eaton
Designer: Lilian Lindblom
Illustrators: Anna Koska, Nadine Wickenden
Contributors: Fiona Barnett, Tessa Evelegh, Pamela Westland
Photography: James Duncan, Michelle Garrett, Debbie Patterson
Jacket Photography: Amanda Heywood

Printed and bound in China

CONTENTS

INTRODUCTION

The vagaries of fashion have had their impact on flower arranging just as they have on most other aspects of life.

However, one discernible long-term trend has been a relaxation of the formal approach of 20 years or more ago, when flowers sometimes looked as though they had been beaten into submission!

Nowadays, the straitjacket of formality has been replaced by an emphasis on the flowers themselves creating the impact in a natural way.

No longer restricted by a set of rigid rules, the flower arranger is free to take inspiration from anything that triggers the creative process, be it the decor of a room or a particular type of container.

Of course, modern flower arranging still relies on the basic principles of colour, scale, proportion and balance but it uses these to create more adventurous designs in exciting colour combinations and textures. It is also concerned with simplicity.

It has become the art of understanding the materials and getting the best out of them with the minimum complication.

One of the single most important factors in allowing the modern flower arranger a great deal more creative freedom has been the enormous improvement in both the availability and the quality of commercially grown cut flowers.

The flower arranger is no longer restricted by the seasonal availability of the majority of popular cut blooms and has an ever-growing range of flowers to work with. Further, modern growing techniques have improved the quality and increased the life span of cut flowers, for example the few days' cut life of the sweet pea has been extended to a week or more.

All of these improvements give today's flower arranger more options in terms of choice of materials, colour palette and arranging techniques.

To some, flower arranging is an all-consuming passion but to many it remains a mystery. In reality, it is an activity in which most people can, to a greater or lesser extent, successfully participate. All you need is a working knowledge of the contents of this book coupled with a little determination, some imagination and lots of practice. The important thing to remember is that flower arranging is a creative, not just a physical, process.

This book is divided into two sections. The first part, *Floral Displays*, presents a wealth of seasonal designs enabling flowers in many shapes and forms to be used throughout the home. In the second part, *Special Occasion Flowers*, there are wonderful ideas for Valentine's Day, weddings and Christmas, as well as fabulous gift ideas for all sorts of occasions.

SPRING BLOSSOM URN

The explosion of plant life in the spring is visually depicted in this arrangement of early flowers and foliage. Heavily flowered heads of white lilac are the focal blossoms of the display set against the dark brown stems of pussy willow and cherry.

MATERIALS

urn
cellophane (plastic wrap)
1´ block plastic foam
scissors
stub (floral) wires
reindeer moss
15 stems pussy willow
10 stems white lilac
15 stems pink cherry blossom

1 Line the urn with cellophane (plastic wrap) and wedge in the water-soaked block of plastic foam. Trim away the excess cellophane.

2 Make hairpins from stub (floral) wires and pin reindeer moss into the plastic foam around the urn rim.

3 Arrange the pussy willow in the urn to establish the height and width of a symmetrical outline.

4 Distribute the lilac throughout the pussy willow.

5 Position the pink cherry blossom throughout the display in order to reinforce the overall shape.

TULIP ARRANGEMENT

Sometimes the simple beauty of an arrangement that relies entirely on one type of flower in its own foliage can be breathtaking. This display of 'Angelique' tulips in glorious profusion contains nothing to compete with their soft pastel pink colour and would make a dramatic room centrepiece.

MATERIALS

50 stems 'Angelique' tulips
watertight container
such as a small bucket
basket
scissors

TIP

The arrangement is technically relatively unstructured but, by repetition of the regular form of the tulip heads, the overall visual effect is that of a formal dome of flowers to be viewed in the round.

1 Strip the lower leaves from the tulips to prevent them from rotting in the water. Fill the bucket with water and place in the basket.

2 Cut each tulip stem to the correct size and place the stems in the water. Start building the display from its outside edge inwards.

3 Continue arranging the tulips towards the centre of the display until a full and even domed shape is achieved. You should be able to view the display from all sides.

THE MODERN APPROACH

A tall, wide cylindrical vase, spatter-painted to harmonize with the wall
behind it, is on just the right lines for a low-key floral display in a modern setting.

MATERIALS

plastic-coated wire
mesh netting
tall, wide cylindrical vase
scissors
florist's adhesive tape
3 stems acanthus leaves
10 stems Lilium longiflorum
5 stems white roses
5 stems cream roses
2 stems eucalyptus
8 stems pampas grass

1 Crumple the wire mesh netting into a ball and fit it into the neck of the container. Cut and thread two lengths of adhesive tape through the netting, criss-cross them over the container and stick the ends close to the rim, where they will be concealed by the lowest of the plant materials. Arrange the acanthus stems so that the leaves form a bowl shape to outline the flowers, with the tallest stems at the back and the shortest ones at the front.

2 Position the lily stems so that the fully opened flowers are pointing in different directions – some forward, some to the right, and some to the left. In this way you can appreciate the full beauty of these flowers in silhouette.

3 Cut off all but the topmost rose leaves. Split the ends of the rose stems to facilitate water intake.

4 Arrange the roses so that they nestle among the lily stems and give an overall roundness to the design. Add eucalyptus sprays to trail over the container rim, and a few strands of pampas grass at one side.

SPRING NAPKIN DECORATION

The sophisticated gold and white colour combination used in these
elegant and delicate napkin decorations would be perfect for a formal dinner.

MATERIALS

small-leaved ivy trails (sprigs)
napkins
scissors
1 pot lily-of-the-valley
1 pot tiny cyclamen
(dwarf Cyclamen persicum*)*
gold cord

1 Wrap an ivy trail (sprig) around the middle of a rolled napkin. Tie the stem in a knot. Using 4–5 stems of lily-of-the-valley and 3 cyclamen flowers on their stems, create a small flat-backed sheaf by spiralling the stems.

2 Place one cyclamen leaf at the back of the lily-of-the-valley for support and place two more around the cyclamen flowers to emphasize the focal point. Tie at the binding point with gold cord. Lay the sheaf on top of the napkin and ivy, wrap gold cord around the napkin and stems, gently tying it into a bow.

TIED POSY

Flowers are at their most appealing when kept simple. Just gather together some garden cuttings and arrange them in a pretty posy that the recipient can simply unwrap and put straight into a vase, without further ado.

MATERIALS
....
secateurs (pruning shears)
5 stems pink roses
10 stems eucalyptus
8 stems scabious
brown paper
ribbon

1 Using secateurs (pruning shears), cut each flower stem to approximately 15 cm (6 in) long. Gather the flowers together, surrounding each rose with some feathery eucalyptus, and then add the scabious.

2 Wrap the posy with paper and tie it with a pretty ribbon bow.

GEOMETRY LESSON

Whoever would have thought, when learning about right-angled triangles,
that the knowledge would be put to use in a flower arrangement!
This design, an interpretation of the classic "L-shape", is composed on a
stoneware dish which has, by contrast, gentle curves.

MATERIALS

scissors
florist's adhesive clay
pinholder
shallow waterproof dish such as
a baking or serving dish
10 stems slender foliage such
as grevillea
5 stems blue irises
5 stems white irises
10 stems daffodils
5 stems anemones ('Mona Lisa' blue)
concealing material such as broken
windscreen (windshield) glass

TIP

Glass has the advantage as a
concealing material – over pebbles
and granite, for example – of catch
ing and reflecting the light in an
attractive way.

1 Cut three short lengths of
florist's adhesive clay and press
on to the bottom of the pinholder.
Position this to one side of the
container and press firmly in place.

2 Define the shape of the "L" with
long, straight stems of foliage
placed at right angles to one another.
Note that the principal upright stem
is a little way in from the edge of the
pinholder. Give balance to the design
by placing a shorter stem to the left
of the principal stem with another
angled to the right.

3 Position the irises, pressing the
stems firmly on to the pinholder
spikes, so that the flowers follow the
shape outlined by the leaves.

4 Position the daffodils to fill in
the gaps and complement the
contrasting shape of the irises. Place
a cluster of short-stemmed anemones
close to the pinholder, where the
flowers will be seen as deep shadows,
and add a few foliage sprays. Spoon
the concealing material – in this case
broken windscreen (windshield) glass
– around the pinholder until it is
completely hidden.

OLD-FASHIONED GARDEN ROSE ARRANGEMENT

The beautiful full-blown blooms of these antique-looking roses give an opulent and romantic feel to a very simple combination of flower and container. This arrangement deserves centre stage in any room setting.

MATERIALS

watertight container, to put inside plant pot
low, weathered terracotta plant pot
jug (pitcher)
variety garden roses, short- and long-stemmed
scissors

TIP

The technique is to mass one type of flower in several varieties whose papery petals will achieve a textural mix of colour and scent.

1 Place the watertight container inside the terracotta plant pot and fill with water. Fill the jug (pitcher) as well. Select and prepare your blooms and remove the lower foliage and thorns.

2 Position the longer-stemmed blooms in the jug (pitcher) with the heads massed together. This ensures that the cut stems are supported and so can simply be placed directly into the water.

3 Mass shorter, more open flower heads in the glass bowl inside the plant pot with the stems hidden and the heads showing just above the rim of the pot. The heads look best if kept either all on one level or in a slight dome shape. If fewer flowers are used, plastic-coated wire mesh netting or plastic foam may be needed to control the positions of individual blooms.

SUMMER BASKET DISPLAY

The lovely scents, luscious blooms and vast range of colours
available in summer provide endless possibilities for creating wonderful displays.
This arrangement is a bountiful basket, overflowing with seasonal summer
blooms, which can be scaled up or down to suit any situation.

MATERIALS

basket
cellophane (plastic wrap)
scissors
2 blocks plastic foam
florist's adhesive tape
10 stems Viburnum tinus
15 stems larkspur in 3 colours
6 stems 'Stargazer' lilies
5 large ivy leaves
10 stems white phlox

1 Line the basket with cellophane (plastic wrap) to prevent leakage, and cut to fit. Then secure the two soaked blocks of plastic foam in the lined basket with the florist's adhesive tape.

2 Arrange the viburnum stems in the plastic foam to establish the overall height, width and shape. Strengthen the outline using the larkspur, making sure you use all of the stems and not just the flower spikes.

TIP
Keep the display well watered and it should go on flowering for at least a week. The lilies should open fully in plastic foam and new phlox buds will keep opening to replace the spent heads.

3 Place the lilies in a diagonal line across the arrangement. Position the large ivy leaves around the lilies in the centre of the display. Arrange the phlox across the arrangement along the opposite diagonal to the lilies.

ALL FOLIAGE ARRANGEMENT

Creating an arrangement entirely from different types of foliage can be both challenging and rewarding. No matter what the season, finding three or four varieties of foliage is not difficult. Anything from the common privet to the most exotic shrubs can be used and to great effect.

MATERIALS

2 blocks plastic foam
large shallow bowl
florist's adhesive tape
scissors
stub (floral) wires
bun moss
5 stems grevillea
10 stems shrimp plant
(Beloperone guttata)
10 stems ming fern
(cultivar of Boston fern)
10 stems Pittosporum
5 stems cotoneaster

1 Soak the plastic foam and secure it in the bowl with florist's adhesive tape.

2 Make U-shaped staples from stub (floral) wire and pin bun moss around the rim of the bowl.

3 Arrange the grevillea to establish the maximum height. Work diagonally across with progressively shorter stems, finishing with foliage flowing over the front of the bowl. Arrange the shrimp plant in a similar way along the opposite diagonal, but make it shorter than the grevillea and emphasize the line by adding ming fern.

4 Intersperse the line of grevillea with the *Pittosporum*. Finally, distribute the cotoneaster evenly throughout the whole arrangement.

COUNTRY STYLE

A medley of cottage-garden flowers vividly contrasting in shape,
texture, and colour are arranged just as they might grow in a border –
intermingled and in profusion.

MATERIALS
....

plastic-coated wire
mesh netting
large jug (pitcher) or vase
florist's adhesive tape
scissors
3 stems Euphorbia fulgens
15 stems goldenrod
6 stems delphiniums
9 stems marigolds

1 Crumple the wire mesh netting into a ball and fit it into the neck of the jug (pitcher) so that it forms a mound above the rim. Criss-cross two pieces of adhesive tape over the wire, threading them through it in places and sticking the ends to the container. Arrange the arched stems of *Euphorbia* so that they droop over the jug handle, on one side only.

2 Arrange the goldenrod stems so that they form a pyramid shape, with the tallest ones in the centre.

3 Position the delphinium stems among the goldenrod and towards the back of the design.

4 Arrange the round, flat-faced marigold flowers at varying heights so that they are seen in a circular formation. Select the best, brightest specimen to place in the centre front, where it will overlap the rim of the jug.

Blue and White Tussie Mussies

*Small, hand-tied spiralled posies make perfect gifts and, in the right vase,
ideal centre decorations for small tables. Both of these displays have
delicate flowers massed together. One features Japanese anemones,
visually strengthened by blackberries on stems; the other delphiniums
supported by rosehip stems.*

MATERIALS

TUSSIE 1 (ON LEFT)
*10 stems white Japanese anemones
blackberries on stems
1 stem draceana
twine
scissors
ribbon*

TUSSIE 2 (ON RIGHT)
*4-5 stems 'Blue Butterfly' delphinium
3 stems rosehips
5 small Virginia creeper leaves
twine
scissors
ribbon*

1 Start with a central flower and add stems of foliage and flowers, turning the posy in your hand to build the design into a spiral.

2 Once all the ingredients have been used, and the bunch is completed, tie firmly at the binding point with twine. Repeat steps one and two for the second tussie mussie.

3 Trim the ends of the flower stems with scissors to achieve a neat edge. Finish both tussie mussies with ribbon bows.

Tip
While the flowers need to be tightly
massed for the best effect, they have
relatively large but fragile blooms, so
take care not to crush their petals,
and tie off firmly but gently.

AUTUMN CROCUS TRUG

Bring the outdoors inside by planting up an old trug with flowering crocus bulbs in soil covered in a natural-looking carpet of moss and leaves. This simple display is as effective as the most sophisticated cut-flower arrangement.

MATERIALS

trug
cellophane (plastic wrap)
soil
6 flowering crocus bulbs
bun moss
autumn leaves
raffia
scissors

1 Line the trug with cellophane (plastic wrap), fill with soil and plant the crocus bulbs. Ensure the bulbs are firmly planted and then water them.

2 Arrange the bun moss on top of the soil, then scatter the leaves over the moss to create a natural-looking, autumnal effect.

TIP
Although one expects to see crocuses in the spring, this beautiful autumn variety is a welcome sight as its flowers push up determinedly through the fallen leaves. Of course, they do not have to be confined to the garden.

3 To finish, tie raffia into bows, and attach one on either side of the base of the trug handle.

HOGARTH CURVE

The design is named after the 18th-century English painter
William Hogarth, who called flowing curves "lines of beauty".
The stems creating the upper and lower curves should be placed so the outline
appears as one rhythmic and unbroken line, sometimes known as a "lazy S".

MATERIALS

scissors
florist's adhesive clay
small waterproof container for
plastic foam
1 block plastic foam, cut to shape
and soaked
knife
florist's adhesive tape
20 stems curved broom
tall, slender container such as
a candlestick
10 stems variegated scented
geranium leaves
5 stems peach carnations
1 stem white spray chrysanthemum
1 stem peach spray carnation
5 stems smilax

*T*IP
It is important to select or coax foliage or flower stems into matching curves to form the outline of the design. These broom stems were twisted into a circle, secured with elastic bands, and left overnight.

1 Cut two short lengths of adhesive clay, press on to the underside of the foam holder and press the holder on top of the container. Position the foam in the container. Tape from side to side and front to back, over the foam and on to the candlestick. Define the S-shape by placing clusters of broom stems exactly opposite each other on either side of the plastic foam. Reinforce the centre of the S-shape with delicate-scented geranium leaves, leaving the tips slender and wispy.

2 Cut the carnation stems short and place one on either side and one low at the centre front of the design, where it will mask the container and holding material.

3 Position two more carnations, one to create a central dome effect and the other at the back of the design. Cut short stems of spray chrysanthemums and position them to fill in the gaps and provide a colour contrast. Add spray carnations to follow the outline of the foliage. Position short sprays of smilax between the principal flowers, with others trailing low at the front and back of the design to mask every trace of the mechanics.

WHITE JAPANESE ANEMONE VASE

This delightful arrangement combining forest fruits and rosehips with garden anemones, though simple in concept, becomes a sumptuous display when placed in this elegant vase.

MATERIALS

vase
scissors
blackberries on stems
rosehips on stems
2 stems white Japanese anemones
'Honorine Jobert'
4 vine leaves

1 Having filled the vase with water, use the blackberry stems to establish the outline shape. Add the stems of rosehips to reinforce both the structure and the visual balance of the display.

2 Add the anemones evenly throughout the arrangement. Take great care with anemones as they are extremely delicate.

TIP

The rosehips and blackberry stalks used here are very prickly; they need careful handling and the thorns need to be stripped. However, these stems form a strong framework to hold the delicate anemones in position. The addition of vine leaves around the neck of the vase provides a finishing touch to the arrangement.

3 Place the stems of the vine leaves in the water so that they form a collar around the base of the arrangement and are visible above the neck of the vase.

ORANGE ARRANGEMENT

*The matt green of salal tips creates the perfect background for the
spectacular zesty orange colour of the flowers used in this display.*

MATERIALS

*wire basket
reindeer moss
cellophane (plastic wrap)
knife
1 block plastic foam
florist's adhesive tape
scissors
10 stems salal tips
7 stems orange lilies
10 stems orange tulips
20 stems marigolds*

1 Line the basket with reindeer moss and line the moss with cellophane (plastic wrap). Cut a block of soaked plastic foam to fit the basket and tape securely in place.

2 Push the salal tips into the plastic foam to create a dome-shaped foliage outline in proportion with the container.

3 Cut the lily stems to a length to suit the foliage framework and push into the foam evenly throughout the arrangement to reinforce the overall shape. Distribute the tulips evenly through the display, remembering they will continue to grow and their natural downward curve will tend to straighten.

4 Add the marigolds last and place them evenly throughout the display.

LILY AND HYACINTH PLANTED BASKET

When the budget is tight, an economic way of creating a large display
with lots of impact is to use plants instead of cut flowers.

MATERIALS

large wire basket
bun or carpet moss
cellophane (plastic wrap)
scissors
3 flowering lily plants (3 stems
per pot), such as 'Mona Lisa'
3 flowering hyacinth bulbs
8 red-barked dogwood (Cornus alba)
branches (or similar)
raffia

1 Line the whole basket with a layer of moss then, in turn, line the moss with cellophane (plastic wrap). Cut to fit.

2 Using the soil from their pots, plant the lilies in the lined basket, with the hyacinth bulbs between them. Cover the soil with moss.

TIP
The branches of the red-barked dogwood are tied with raffia to form a decorative and supportive structure around the arrangement. A more formal look can be achieved by substituting bamboo canes, tied perhaps with strips of velvet in rich colours.

3 Push four branches of dogwood through the moss and into the soil to form a square around the plants. Cross those horizontally with four more branches, tying them together with raffia to create a frame, then trim the raffia.

ARUM LILY VASE

*Pure in colour and form, elegant and stately, the arum lily has
the presence to be displayed on its own, supported by the minimum of
well-chosen foliage. Here it is arranged with the wonderfully
contorted willow and the large, simple leaves of aucuba, which serve
purely as a backdrop to the beauty of the arum.*

MATERIALS

*vase
branches of contorted willow
scissors
6 arum lilies
2 bushy branches aucuba 'Gold Dust'*

1 Fill the vase to approximately
three-quarters full with water.
Arrange the contorted willow in the
vase to establish the overall height of
the arrangement. (When cutting a
willow stem to the right length, cut
the base at a 45° angle and scrape
the bark off to approximately 5 cm
(2 in) from the end, then split this
section.)

TIP
The choice of container is of great
importance, the visual requirement
being for simple unfussy shapes, with
glass and metal being particularly
appropriate. The chosen vase should
complement the sculptural impact
of the arum.

2 Arrange the arum lilies at
different heights throughout the
willow to achieve a visual balance.
The willow stems will help support
the blooms. Give visual substance
to the display by adding stems of
aucuba throughout to provide a
dark backdrop to throw the arum
blooms into sharp relief.

FRESH VALENTINE TERRACOTTA POTS

With luck, Valentine's Day brings with it red roses, but these small
jewel-like arrangements present them in an altogether different way.
The deep red of the roses visually links the two pots: contrasting with the
acid lime green of 'Santini' chrysanthemums in one, and combining richly
with purple phlox in the other.

MATERIALS
....

half block plastic foam
2 small terracotta pots, 1 slightly
larger than the other
cellophane (plastic wrap)
knife
scissors
ming fern
ivy leaves
5 stems 'Santini' spray
chrysanthemums
6 stems purple phlox
18 stems dark red roses

1 Soak the plastic foam in water. Line both terracotta pots with cellophane (plastic wrap). Cut the foam into small blocks and wedge into the lined pots. Then trim the cellophane to fit. Do not trim too close to the edge of the pot.

2 Build a dome-shaped foliage outline in proportion to each pot. In the larger pot, push the stems of ming fern into the plastic foam and in the small pot push the ivy leaves into the foam.

3 In the larger pot, arrange 'Santini' chrysanthemums amongst the ming fern. In the small pot, distribute the purple phlox amongst the ivy to emphasize the dome shapes of both.

4 Strip the leaves from the dark red roses, cut the stems to the desired lengths and arrange evenly throughout both displays.

DAFFODIL WOOD

*This Easter arrangement evokes one of the loveliest harbingers of spring –
the sight of golden daffodils making a bright floral carpet under the bare
branches of an apple tree. The arrangement could be positioned in
a church porch, on the floor, or on a low wooden chest.*

MATERIALS

*large flat plate
large flat woven tray, about
40 cm (16 in) diameter
scissors
florist's adhesive clay
2 plastic prongs
plastic foam, cut to size and
then soaked
knife
piece of well-shaped wood,
such as vinewood
stub (floral) wires
sphagnum moss
20 stems daffodils
30 stems narcissuses
10 ivy trails (sprigs)
5 short stems pussy willow
with catkins*

TIP

If you are not fortunate enough to
find a shapely piece of wood in the
countryside, you could use a handful
of gnarled twigs – apple would be
ideal.

1 Place the plate or other solid
waterproof liner in the tray. Cut
two strips of adhesive clay and press
them on to the underside of both
plastic prongs. Press them in position
well apart on the liner, where they
will anchor the main blocks of foam.
Press two large pieces of foam on to
the spikes and cut other pieces to fill
in the circle around the edges. Cut a
hole in the foam, towards the back
and at one side, and push the
vinewood into it. Twist two or three
wires around the wood, twist the
ends and press them at different
angles into the foam, so that the
"tree" is held firmly in place.

2 Cover the foam with a thin layer
of moss. Scrape away just
enough of the moss to expose small
areas, and press the daffodil stems
vertically into the foam. Cut them to
slightly varying heights to give the
most natural effect.

3 Cut shorter stems of narcissus and arrange them in a group in front of the daffodils. Position stems of ivy to twine around the vinewood and trail through a clump of daffodils. Position short sprays of ivy around the rim to edge and enclose the design and arrange a few pussy willow stems with catkins to provide shape and texture variation.

CELEBRATION TABLE DECORATION

A table for any celebratory lunch will not usually have much room
to spare on it. In this instance, there is no room for the wine cooler,
and the answer is to incorporate it within the flower arrangement.
The floral decoration is a sumptuous, textural display of gold, yellow
and white flowers with green and grey foliage.

MATERIALS

40 cm (16 in) diameter plastic
foam ring
scissors
12 stems Senecio laxifolius
15 stems elaeagnus
3 groups of 2 chestnuts
stub (floral) wires
thick gloves
18 stems yellow roses
10 stems cream-coloured
Eustoma grandiflorum
10 stems solidago
10 stems fennel

1 Soak the plastic foam ring in water. Cut the senecio to a stem length of around 14 cm (5½ in) and distribute evenly around the ring, pushing the stems into the plastic foam. Leave the centre of the ring clear.

3 Double leg mount three groups of two chestnuts on stub (floral) wire and cut the wire legs to about 6 cm (2¼ in). Take care, as the chestnuts are extremely prickly. It is advisable to wear thick gardening gloves when handling them. Position the chestnuts at three equidistant points around the circumference of the plastic foam ring, and secure by pushing the wires into the foam.

2 Cut the elaeagnus to a length of 14 cm (5½ in) and distribute evenly throughout the senecio to reinforce the foliage outline.

4 Cut the rose stems to about 14 cm (5½ in) in length and arrange in staggered groups of three roses at six points around the ring, equal distances apart, pushing the stems firmly into the foam.

5 Cut stems of eustoma flower heads 12 cm (4¾ in) long from the main stem. Arrange the stems evenly in the foam. Cut the stems of solidago to a length of about 14 cm (5½ in) and distribute throughout. Finally, cut the stems of fennel to about 12 cm (4¾ in) long and add evenly throughout the display.

SCENTED BASKET

A young bridesmaid may find it easier to carry a basket than clutch a posy
during a seemingly endless wedding ceremony.
This basket uses simple flowers, in a simple colour combination,
simply arranged. The result is a beautiful display appropriate for
a child bridesmaid or a Mother's Day gift.

MATERIALS

small basket
cellophane (plastic wrap)
scissors
quarter block plastic foam
knife
florist's adhesive tape
ribbon
silver wires
20 10 cm (4 in) stems golden privet
6 stems tuberose
20 stems 'Grace' freesias

1 Line the basket with cellophane (plastic wrap), and trim to fit. Soak the plastic foam in water, trim to fit into the basket, and secure in the centre with florist's adhesive tape. Form two small bows from the ribbon. Tie around their centres with silver wires and attach them to the basket, leaving the excess wire projecting at their back. Bind the handle of the basket with ribbon, securing it at either end by tying around the wire tails of the bows.

2 Build a domed outline to the arrangement with the golden privet, cut to the appropriate length.

3 Cut the tuberose stems to about 9 cm (3½ in) and position in a staggered diagonal across the basket.

4 Cut the freesia stems to around 9 cm (3½ in) long and space evenly throughout the basket. Recess some heads to give greater depth to the finished display.

TIED BRIDAL BOUQUET

*This classic "shower" wedding bouquet has a generous trailing shape
and incorporates* Lilium longiflorum *as its focal flowers, using the
traditional, fresh bridal colour combination of white, cream and green.*

MATERIALS

10 stems Lilium longiflorum
10 stems cream Eustoma grandiflorum
10 stems white Euphorbia fulgens
5 stems Molucella laevis
10 stems white aster 'Monte Cassino'
10 stems dill
10 ivy trails (sprigs)
twine
scissors
raffia

1 Hold one lily stem in your hand about 25 cm (10 in) down from the top of its flower head. Begin adding the other flowers and ivy trails (sprigs) in a regular sequence to get an even distribution of materials throughout the bouquet. As you do this, keep turning the bunch in your hand to make the stems form a spiral.

2 To one side of the bouquet add materials on longer stems than the central flower – these will form the trailing element of the display. To the opposite side, add stems slightly shorter than the central bloom, and this will become the top of the bouquet.

3 When you have finished the bouquet and are satisfied with the shape, tie it with twine at the binding point, firmly, but not too tightly. Cut the stems so that they are 12 cm (4¾ in) long below the binding point. Any shorter and the weight of the bouquet will not be distributed evenly and it will make it difficult to carry.

 4 Tie raffia around the binding point and form a bow which sits on top of the stems, facing upwards towards the person carrying the bouquet.

TIP

A bouquet of this size requires quite a large quantity of material, which may prove expensive, but the design lends itself to being scaled down to suit a tighter budget by using the same materials in smaller quantities.

BABY BIRTH GIFT

Celebrate a baby's birth by giving the parents this very pretty arrangement in an unusual but practical container. The display incorporates double tulips, ranunculus, phlox and spray roses, with small leaves of Pittosporum. *It is the delicacy of the flowers and foliage which make it appropriate for a baby.*

MATERIALS

1 block plastic foam
knife
small galvanized metal bucket
scissors
1 bunch Pittosporum
15 stems pale pink 'Angelique' tulips
5 stems white spray roses
10 stems white ranunculus
10 stems white phlox
1 bunch dried lavender
ribbon

TIP

The choice of soft subtle colours means it is suitable for either a boy or girl. There is also the added bonus of the beautiful scent of phlox and dried lavender.

1 Soak the plastic foam in water, cut it to fit the small metal bucket and wedge it firmly in place. Cut the *Pittosporum* to a length of 12 cm (4¾ in) and clean the leaves from the lower part of the stems. Push the stems into the plastic foam to create an overall domed foliage outline within which the flowers can be arranged.

2 Cut the 'Angelique' tulips to a stem length of 10 cm (4 in) and distribute them evenly throughout the foliage. Cut individual off-shoots from the main stems of the spray roses to a length of 10 cm (4 in), and arrange throughout the display, with full blooms at the centre and buds around the outside.

3 Cut the ranunculus and phlox to a stem length of 10 cm (4 in) and distribute both throughout the display. Cut the lavender to a stem length of 12 cm (4¾ in) and arrange in groups of three stems evenly throughout the flowers and foliage. Tie the ribbon around the bucket and finish in a generous bow.

GOLDEN WEDDING BOUQUET

This shimmering bouquet makes an unequivocal Golden Wedding statement. Unashamed in its use of yellows and golds, the colours are carried right through the design in the flowers, the wrapping paper, the twine and the ribbon, even to a fine sprinkling of gold dust.

MATERIALS

20 stems golden yellow ranunculus
20 stems mimosa
gold twine
scissors
2 sheets gold-coloured tissue paper in 2 shades
piece gold-coloured fabric about 46 cm (18 in) long, 15 cm (6 in) wide
gold dust glitter

TIP

The arrangement makes a flamboyant gift but nonetheless is as simple to create as a hand-tied bouquet. It can be unwrapped and placed straight into a vase of water, with no need for further arranging.

1 Lay out the stems of ranunculus and mimosa so that they are easily accessible. Clean the stems of leaves from about a third of the way down. Holding a stem of ranunculus in your hand, build the bouquet by adding alternate stems of mimosa and ranunculus, turning the flowers in your hand all the while so that the stems form a spiral.

2 When all the flowers have been arranged in your hand, tie the stems together at the binding point with the gold twine. When secured, trim the stems to a length about one-third of the overall height of the finished bouquet.

3 Wrap the bouquet in two shades of tissue paper, and tie the gold twine around the binding point. Then tie a bow of gold fabric around the binding point. To finish, sprinkle gold dust over the flowers.

Party Piece

Flowers arranged for a buffet party or a special family celebration can use artistic licence in the matter of colour, break some of the rules and earn nothing but praise. This party piece proves that you can blend red, blue, orange, mauve, yellow and green – all the colours of the rainbow – in an arrangement that will command attention across a crowded room.

MATERIALS

florist's adhesive clay
1 plastic prong
footed glass or china dish such as a cake stand
plastic foam, soaked in water
scissors
10 stems foliage such as eucalyptus and grevillea
15 stems Peruvian lilies
6 stems Singapore orchids
5 stems blue irises
5 stems pale-coloured roses
6 stems mixed carnations

TIP

This is an occasion when you can give way to the temptation to choose several bunches of flowers of different types, colours, shapes and sizes. Cut all the stem ends at a sharp angle to facilitate the intake of water, and give the flowers a long drink in cool water before arranging them.

1 Stick a piece of adhesive clay to the underside of the plastic prong and press on to the container slightly behind the centre point. Press the soaked foam on to the spikes of the prong. Arrange the various types of foliage to make a fan shape across the centre of the arrangement, and to cascade down over the rim of the container at the front and sides.

2 Arrange the Peruvian lilies – here deep coral, peach and cream colours were used – to follow the outline of the foliage. Cut some of the individual flowers on short stems and position them close to the foam.

3 Arrange the orchid stems in a triangular shape throughout the design, the tallest stem upright in the centre and progressively shorter stems slanted outwards at the front. If you cut the stems short and have to cut off some of the lower florets, position these as attractive "fillers" close to the foam.

4 Arrange the irises to make a
patch of contrasting colour – the
only blue in the design – at the back.
Cut the stems at a sharply slanting
angle. The sword-like leaves can be
used at the back of the arrangement.
Turn the container around and fill in
the back of the design with sprays of
foliage and a selection of flowers to
give the arrangement depth and
perspective.

5 Complete the arrangement by
adding the softening influence of
the roses and carnations, which
contrast well with the trumpet- and
star-like shapes of the other flowers.
Add more foliage to fill in any gaps,
and check that the design looks good
from both sides.

FIT FOR A BRIDE

For a close friend or a relative of the bride it is both a pleasure and
a privilege to compose the bridal bouquet. Confirm her preference for
flower types and colours, then follow our easy step-by-step instructions for
a bouquet fit for the most discerning bride.

MATERIALS

stub (floral) wires
wire cutters
white floral tape
florist's silver roll wire
scissors
Singapore orchids
Peruvian lilies
freesias
irises
narcissus
roses
mimosa
ballota and pampas grass
satin ribbon

1 It is essential to wire flowers for a bouquet of this kind, otherwise the bundle of stems forming the handle would both look and feel clumsy. Cut short the flower stems and push a stub (floral) wire into the ends. Bind over the join and down along the wire with overlapping white floral tape.

TIP

Design the bride's bouquet to feature the flowers and colours that will set the scene for the ceremony and the reception and complement the colours she and her attendants will wear. If the bride's dress is in off-white or cream, avoid using pure white flowers which would be unflattering to the fabric. Give all the flowers a long drink of cool water in a shady place before composing the bouquet.

2 Gather together all the flowers that will form the centre of the bouquet – orchids, Peruvian lilies, freesias, irises, narcissus and a rose – and bind the false wire stems with silver roll wire.

3 Hold the core of the bouquet in one hand and arrange slender stems of foliage to cascade over the flowers. Arrange a second layer of flowers around the front and sides of the central ones and bind all the stems and false stems with silver roll wire.

4 Arrange a third layer of flowers around the front and sides of the bouquet, bind the stems with silver roll wire, and add a few feature flowers close to the grip. Roses and short sprays of mimosa look good in this position. Bind the stems again with wire, and then with the satin ribbon, tying it just under the lowest of the flowers. Tie the ribbon in a bow and leave long, trailing ends. Spray the flowers with a fine mist of cool water, and keep in a cool place.

FRESH FLOWERS AS A GIFT-WRAP DECORATION

This flower decoration offers the opportunity to make a gift extra special,
and to give flowers at the same time. The colour and form of the gerbera
and 'Mona Lisa' lily heads are very bold, and this is contrasted with the
small delicate bell heads of lily-of-the-valley.

MATERIALS

1 stem 'Mona Lisa' lily
scissors
1 branch lichen-covered larch
1 small pot lily-of-the-valley
2 stems pink gerbera
raffia
gift-wrapped present
ribbon

TIP

The decoration is made as a small, tied, flat-based sheaf. This involves no wiring and thus is relatively simple to make, provided you give sufficient thought to the visual balance between the bold and delicate elements.

1 From the lily stem, cut a 20 cm (8 in) length with one bud and one open flower on it. Also cut a single open flower on an 8 cm (3¼ in) stem. Cut six twigs from the larch branch, each about 25 cm (10 in) long. Cut three lily-of-the-valley on stems approximately 15 cm (6 in) long, each with a leaf. Cut one gerbera stem to 18 cm (7 in) long and the second to 14 cm (5½ in) long. Create a flat fan-shaped outline with the larch twigs. Position the longer lily stem in the centre of the fan and the shorter single one below.

Next arrange the lily-of-the-valley and gerbera around the two lilies. Tie the stems securely with raffia at the point where they all cross.

2 Lay the completed decoration diagonally across the wrapped gift. Take a long piece of raffia around the flowers, crossing under the parcel and bringing it back up to tie off on top of the stems.

Wrap the ribbon around the binding point of the decoration and tie a bow.

WEDDING DECORATION

*Hanging decorations in a church or chapel complement the larger
arrangements, the pedestal and windowsill designs, and further enhance
the setting for a wedding or baptism. Such decorations may hang on the ends
of pews, or on pillars, posts and altar screens.*

MATERIALS

*small block plastic foam, soaked
in water
plastic foam-holding tray, with handle
florist's adhesive tape (optional)
4 stems grevillea
8 stems broom
a few stems variegated leaves and
flowering shrub
2 stems carnations
4-5 stems mixed irises
8-10 stems Peruvian lilies
2 stems white spray carnations
scissors
6 mm (¼ in) wide ribbon
stub (floral) wires
wire cutters
ribbon
wire or twine for hanging*

TIP

If making more than one decoration,
divide the flowers and foliage
into groups before you start the
arrangements, so that they all match
one another.

1 Press a slice cut from a block
of soaked foam into the plastic
holder. Hold the container vertically,
and check that the foam is held
firmly in place. If necessary, tape it
in place with two strips of florist's
adhesive tape. Arrange long stems of
slender foliage at the top and bottom
of the holder and shorter sprays in
the centre.

2 Cut short a carnation stem and
position it just above the centre
of the foam. Arrange the irises above
and below it. Cut individual Peruvian
lily flowers and arrange them to
form the background of the design.

3 Arrange sprays of foliage and
shrub to isolate some of the
flowers. Extend the outline with
spray carnations. Cut the narrow
ribbon into three lengths, double
each one, and tie into a bow. Thread
a stub (floral) wire through the back
of the loop and press into the foam.
Make 3 bows from the other ribbon
in the same way and position them
at the base of the decoration.

CHRISTMAS CANDLE TABLE DECORATION

This rich display is a visual feast of the seasonal reds and greens of anemones, ranunculus and holly, softened by the grey of lichen on larch twigs and aromatic rosemary. The simple white candles are given a festive lift with their individual bows.

MATERIALS

25 cm (10 in) diameter plastic foam ring
25 cm (10 in) diameter wire basket with candleholders
10 stems rosemary
10 small stems lichen-covered larch
10 small stems holly
scissors
30 stems red anemones ('Mona Lisa')
30 stems red ranunculus
paper ribbon
4 candles

TIP

The space at the centre of the design is the perfect spot for hiding those little, last-minute surprise presents!

Never leave burning candles unattended and do not allow the candles to burn below 5 cm (2 in) of the display height.

1 Soak the plastic foam ring in water and wedge it snugly into the wire basket. You may need to trim the ring slightly, but make sure that you do not cut too much off by mistake.

2 Using a combination of rosemary, larch and holly, create an even but textured foliage and twig outline, all around the plastic foam ring. Make sure that the various foliages towards the outside edge of the display are shorter than those towards the centre.

3 Cut the stems of the anemones and ranunculus to 7.5 cm (3 in). Arrange them evenly throughout the display, leaving a little space around the candleholders. Make four ribbon bows and attach them to the candles. Position the candles in the holders.

CHRISTMAS ANEMONE URN

This vibrant display uses fabulously rich colours as an alternative to the traditional reds and greens of Christmas. An audacious combination of shocking orange roses set against the vivid purple anemones and the metallic blue berries of laurustinus makes an unforgettable impression.

MATERIALS

*1 small cast-iron urn
cellophane (plastic wrap)
1 block plastic foam
florist's adhesive tape
scissors
1 bunch laurustinus with berries
10 stems bright orange roses
20 stems anemones ('Mona Lisa' blue)*

1 Line the urn with the cellophane (plastic wrap). Soak the plastic foam in water, fit into the lined urn and secure with adhesive tape. Trim the cellophane (plastic wrap) to fit.

2 Clean the stems of laurustinus and evenly arrange in the plastic foam to create a domed, all-round foliage framework within which the flowers will be positioned.

3 Distribute the roses, the focal flowers, evenly throughout the foliage, placing those with the most open blooms about two-thirds of the way up the arrangement.

4 Push the stems of anemones into the plastic foam amongst the roses, spreading them throughout the arrangement so that a domed and regular shape is achieved.

TIP

The classic feel of a Christmas arrangement is retained by the use of the rusting cast-iron urn in which this spectacular display is set.

INDEX